Exploring
THE PACIFIC NORTHWEST

Rose Blue and Corinne J. Naden

Raintree
Chicago, Illinois

Library of Congress Cataloging-in-Publication Data
Blue, Rose.
  Exploring the Pacific Northwest / Rose Blue and
Corinne J. Naden.
      v. cm. -- (Exploring the Americas)
Includes bibliographical references (p.) and index.
Contents: Prologue: who found it? -- Vitus Bering
(1728, 1741): not one continent but two -- Alexander
Mackenzie (1789, 1793): in the far Northwest --
George Vancouver (1791-94): mapping the coast --
Robert Gray (1792): a claim on Oregon -- Meriwether
Lewis and William Clark: the great overland expedi-
tion (1804-06) -- Zebulon Pike: where does the river
begin? (1805-06) -- Manuel Lisa: across the wide
Missouri (1807) -- Peter Skene Ogden: tough man in
the Northwest (1824-30) -- Epilogue: what did they
find? -- Important dates in the exploration of the
Pacific Northwest.
  ISBN 0-7398-4950-6 (HC), 1-4109-0044-4 (Pbk.)
1. Northwest, Pacific--Discovery and exploration--
Juvenile literature. 2. Explorers--Northwest, Pacific--
Biography--Juvenile literature. [1. Northwest, Pacific--
Discovery an d exploration. 2. Explorers.] I. Naden,
Corinne J. II. Title.
III. Series: Blue, Rose. Exploring the Americas.
F851.5 .B57 2003
979.5'01--dc21
                            2002013354

Acknowledgments
The author and publishers are grateful to the following for permission to reproduce copyright material:

Cover photographs by Bettmann/Corbis, (map)
Corbis

pp. 4, 11, 34, 36, 45B, 48, 50, 52 The Granger
Collection, NY; pp. 6L, 18, 19 Bettmann/Corbis;
p. 6R Archivo Iconografico, S.A./Corbis; p. 7 Jacques
Langevin/Corbis SYGMA; p. 8 Natalie Fobes/Corbis;
p. 10 Tom Bean/Corbis; p. 12 The Newberry
Library/Stock Montage, Inc.; p. 13 John
Foster/Masterfile; pp. 14, 28 Corbis; p. 16 David S.
Boyer/National Geographic Society Image Collection;
p. 17 Gunter Marx Photography/Corbis; pp. 20, 40,
42, 45T North Wind Picture Archives; p. 21 Hulton
Archive/Getty Images; p. 22 Charles W.
Campbell/Corbis; pp. 23, 25 Neil Rabinowitz/Corbis;
p. 24 Danny Lehman/Corbis; p. 26 Francis G.
Mayer/Corbis; p. 27 Wolfgang Kaehler/Corbis; p. 29
Raymond Gehman/Corbis; p. 30 James A.
Sugar/Corbis; p. 31 Sanford/Agliolo/Corbis; p. 32
Independence National Historical Park; p. 35 Stock
Montage, Inc.; p. 38 Missouri Historical Society, St.
Louis; p. 39 NASA/Corbis; p. 41 Will Kincaid/AP
Wide World Photo; p. 43 The Newark Museum/Art
Resource, NY; p. 44 Lowell Georgia/Corbis; p. 47
National Portrait Gallery, Smithsonian Institution/Art
Resource, NY; p. 51 James L. Amos/Corbis; p. 56
Oregon Historical Society, #OrHi707

Photo research by Dawn Friedman

Every effort has been made to contact copyright
holders of any material reproduced in this book.
Any omissions will be rectified in subsequent printings
if notice is given to the publisher.

Some words are shown in bold, like **this**. You can
find out what they mean by looking in the Glossary.

Contents

Prologue:

Who Found It?

This story of exploration takes place in the 1700s and early 1800s. Exploration, especially in the American Northwest, was changing. In the years following the voyages of Columbus in the late 1400s, voyage after voyage headed for the Atlantic coasts of the Americas. These explorers sought the riches of what Europeans called the New World, gold and silver and other gems. They claimed land for the home country, which eventually brought settlers to these continents. And, most of all, they looked for a Northwest Passage, a quicker route to the legendary trading wealth of the Far East.

Centuries passed and little by little the explorers began to realize that this new land was far larger than they had imagined. By 1806, about 320,000 people had emigrated to eastern Canada. Farther south, the small colonies established on the Atlantic coast became a nation called the United States. During the presidency of Thomas Jefferson (1801–1809), the country totaled 17 states. All of them were on the eastern side of the Mississippi River. There was much left to explore.

Many explorers of the Pacific Northwest had one important goal: the fur trade. The enormous wilderness of western America seemed to promise a **bonanza** to traders in furs. Danish-born Vitus Bering, working for Russia, was also

This map of the Pacific Northwest was created in the mid to late 1700s.

looking for furs and in the process proved that Asia and North America were separate continents. George Vancouver's maps showed that there was no Northwest Passage to the Far East. This fact was of little importance to those explorers who could establish fur-trading posts, and those who could trade with or subdue the Native Americans who lived there. In many cases the knowledge and skills of the native peoples in the northwest were of great help to these explorers.

To be sure, the new explorers came upon marvelous sights in their travels—mountains and lakes and rivers that bear their names. Alexander Mackenzie traced the course of the Canadian river named for him. Robert Gray sailed the Columbia River in the northwest. Manuel Lisa explored the Missouri River. Peter Ogden traveled the Great Salt Lake region. Some of these men were fur traders and a different breed of explorer as well. Perhaps they were no less brave, daring, or cruel than Columbus himself or Ponce de Leon. Yet, the times were changing and the explorers changed with them.

Meriwether Lewis and William Clark, America's most famous explorers, were different, too. In one way, they were much like the earliest adventurers. Like Columbus or Henry Hudson before them, Lewis and Clark were sent out by the government. Their expedition was President Thomas Jefferson's brainchild. He asked them to find a trade route to the Pacific, to make scientific observations, to work for peace with Native Americans, and to gather information about the vast uncharted lands that lay between the Mississippi River and the Pacific Ocean. Between 1804 and 1806, that is just what Lewis and Clark did.

Zebulon Pike was on a mission for the government, too. He was sent to find the headwaters of the Mississippi River.

He was unsuccessful, but he did gather a great deal of information about the territory. In the process he tried but failed to climb a mountain in the Rockies that was later named for him.

Explorers such as these did truly open a new world, although they did not really "discover" anything. They were not, in most cases, the first to see a particular lake or climb a particular mountain. But they did bring back details of their expeditions, charts and maps, and strange plants, and almost unbelievable tales of a most glorious wilderness. Even more, as in the case of Lewis and Clark, they brought back such detailed journals that the average American could now read about a land that must have seemed a world away.

That, after all, is the real importance of explorers, from the earliest European voyages across the Atlantic Ocean to the first astronaut on the moon or beyond. These were not superhuman people, not superintelligent, or more honest or kind than most. But they were bold enough and curious enough to go into strange, unknown, and even dangerous places. Their journeys make wonderful and exciting adventure stories.

Explorers such as the eight men in this book changed the North American continent. They did not discover it, but they did change it. Along with the adventure, that is surely reason enough for people today to want to know them.

Chapter One
Vitus Bering
Not One Continent, but Two (1728, 1741)

His name is well known in the world of exploration, especially in the far northwest. Vitus Jonassen Bering (1681–1741), a Dane working in the service of Russia, was the first European to map the coast of Alaska. He proved that Asia and America were separate continents. The body of water that flows between the two continents—the Bering **Strait**—is named for him. Bering also helped to pave the way for Russian fur trade into North America. Rather than a dashing adventurer, however, Bering was more of a methodical plodder who painstakingly carried out the instructions of Russian Czar Peter the Great.

In the service of the czar

Little is know about Bering's early life, except that he was born in Horsens, Denmark, and went to sea as a young man, which took him on a voyage to the East Indies. In 1703, he moved to Russia where he married and enlisted in the newly formed Russian navy, joining the fleet of Peter the Great (1672–1725) as a sublieutenant.

He served in **campaigns** in the Baltic, Black, and White Seas during the Great Northern War with Sweden (1700–1721), earning the rank of captain second class in 1720. But when he was refused promotion to captain first class, Bering retired from the navy.

A wood cut of Vitus Bering (1681–1741)

An oil painting of Peter the Great (1672–1725)

In the early years of the 1700s, Russia was thinking about establishing colonies in North America. It also wanted to find a northeast passage, a sea route to China around Siberia. Actually, back in 1648, Semyon Dezhnyov, a Russian, had already sailed through what is now the Bering Strait. It separates Russia and Alaska at the point where the two continents of Asia and North America are closest. However, no one took any notice of his report until 1736, eight years after Bering's first expedition.

Now, Peter the Great wanted to find out just how large his country really was and about its relationship to North America. So, remembering Bering's bravery during the Great Northern War, he recalled the Dane to duty, with the rank of captain first class. Bering would lead the great expedition of discovery.

On February 5, 1725, Bering left St. Petersburg, Russia, with 100 men under his command and Lieutenants Aleksei Chirikov and Martin Spanberg as his assistants. They carried supplies and materials with them to build a boat. Picking up laborers as he went, Bering trekked over 6,000 miles (9,656 kilometers) of Siberian wilderness to reach Okhotsk on the Pacific coast on September 30, 1726. The first phase of the expedition had taken 19 months.

The Bering Strait, which separates Alaska and Russia, is 53 miles (84 kilometers) wide at its narrowest point.

A boat he called the *Fortune* was built at Okhotsk and was used to ferry men and supplies across the Sea of Okhotsk to the Kamchatka Peninsula. Then they sledded across the entire peninsula to the eastern coast, where they built another boat, the *Gabriel*.

It took three and a half years after leaving St. Petersburg for Bering just to begin his mission.

The expedition left the Kamchatka Peninsula on July 13, 1728. Hugging the shoreline, the *Gabriel* sailed toward the northeast corner of Asia and through the narrow strait that now bears his

Pack ice chokes the waters around St. Lawrence Island, Alaska.

name into the Arctic Ocean. He did see a large island farther out to sea, which he called St. Lawrence. It still has the same name but now belongs to Alaska. Because Bering could see that the Asian shore curved to the west and there was no land to the north, he concluded he had reached the tip of Asia and his job was done. Chirikov wanted to push on to make sure the Asian coast did not turn eastward. Spanberg, however, argued that it was already mid-August and they should turn back before they were stuck in the ice for the winter. Bering agreed.

On August 16, the *Gabriel* turned back. The day was foggy. Had it been clear, Bering would have seen the westernmost point of North America and he would have known for sure that he was sailing through a **strait.**

The expedition spent the winter of 1728–1729 on Kamchatka. During those months, he heard from native peoples that there was land to the east, but he made no sightings. Early in the new year he made his way back to Okhotsk and eventually back to St. Petersburg, which he reached in March 1730. He had been gone for five years.

The great northern expedition

Bering was pleased with himself and was convinced he had shown that Asia and America were separate continents. His critics disagreed. They said he should have followed Chirikov's advice. His voyage proved nothing. Stung by attacks on his courage and initiative, Bering proposed a second expedition.

But what began as his fairly modest idea for a more detailed voyage was soon vastly inflated by the Russian authorities. During the reign of Empress Anna (1730–1740), niece of Peter the Great, it evolved into what was called the Great Northern Expedition (1733–1743). Bering was ordered to locate and map the American coast as far as the first European settlement. Other groups under his direction would map the Siberian coast and prove for certain whether Asia and America were one continent or two. Added to all that, Bering was supposed to see what he could do about starting some economic development in Siberia.

Looking back, the task seemed hopeless from the start. Bering, with the new rank of captain commander, was given total responsibility for this vast undertaking and less than total authority over his subordinates. The expedition was cumbersome to say the least. It involved about 3,000 crew members, 13 ships, 5 surveyors, 30 scientists with several hundred books, two landscape painters, and 9 wagonloads of instruments. The first group left St. Petersburg in early 1733.

The entire **trek** across Siberia took three years It was a nightmare of in-fighting among the officers for control, and stubbornness from the scientists. When the group finally arrived in Okhotsk, making the necessary preparations for the expedition to Kamchatka took a long time.

Bering left Okhotsk in September 1740 and sailed across the sea to the eastern coast of Kamchatka where a winter base was established. Called Petropavlovsk, it is today the largest Russian city on Kamchatka. Just getting there was exhausting, and Bering was not ready to begin the expedition until June 4, 1741, when he left Kamchatka in the *St. Peter* with several of the scientists. Chirikov followed in the *St. Paul*. The two ships sailed toward North America but almost immediately lost contact with each other because of stormy weather. Chirikov sailed on alone and reached North America, exploring several Aleutian

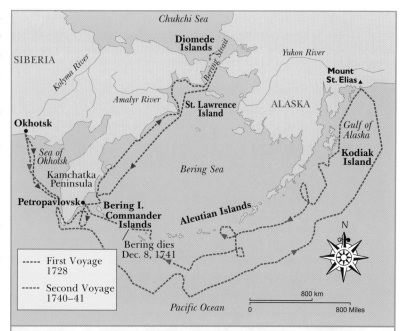

The explorations of Vitus Bering gave Russia a foothold in North America.

Islands. But he lost two of his ship's boats and was fortunate to get back to Kamchatka by October.

The final voyage

Continuing alone, Bering sailed east and north into the Gulf of Alaska. He made brief landings on the coast throughout July and sighted Mount St. Elias on the Alaskan mainland on July 17. His scientific officer Georg Wilhelm Steller, a German naturalist, proposed wintering in Alaska, but Bering ignored his advice. He was weary, exhausted, and anxious to return home. He thought there was time to reach their haven at Petropavlovsk.

Bering might have been able to fight the elements on his journey home, but he could not fight **scurvy.** Scurvy is one of the oldest known human illnesses, caused by a lack of vitamin C (ascorbic acid). It loosens teeth and results in joint stiffness and bleeding under the skin. Untreated, it is fatal. Vitamin C is found in fresh fruits, particularly citrus, and in vegetables. Because sailors at sea in the early centuries had little access to fruits and vegetables on long voyages, they often developed scurvy and many died. For a long time, no one even knew what caused the disease. It was not until 1753 that a Scottish surgeon, James Lind, discovered that scurvy could be prevented or cured by eating oranges, lemons, or limes. British sailors were soon sent to sea with barrels of limes; hence, their nickname, "limeys."

By the end of August, Bering was so ill from scurvy that he could barely leave his cabin. His crew members began to die. Without his command, the ship sailed erratically southwestward and was wrecked on one of the barren Commander Islands early in November. Bering did not know it, of course, but he was only about 300 miles (483 kilometers) from Petropavlovsk.

Bering and the remaining crew spent a ghastly winter living in driftwood huts. Vitus Bering died on December 8, 1741. Thirty others died with him. They were buried on the island that now bears his name.

At 18,008 feet (5,489 meters) Mount St. Elias is the second-highest peak in the United States.

Bering died of scurvy on an island off Siberia.

The following summer, the 45 survivors out of a crew of 77 officers and men built a new boat from the wreckage of the *St. Peter.* They sailed to Petropavlovsk, which they reached on August 27, 1742. There they were greeted by Chirikov.

The graves of Bering and five seamen were uncovered in August 1991 and the remains transported to Moscow, Russia, where they were examined. The following year Bering and his men were reburied on Bering Island.

The expedition of Vitus Bering showed without doubt that North America and Asia were separate continents. It also charted the Siberian coast from the White Sea to the Kolyma River and the American coast from Prince of Wales Island to the Commander Islands. In addition, the tales of a land rich in furs started a steady stream of Russian trappers to Alaska, thus giving Russia a toehold on land claims in Alaska. Although Bering was criticized by Steller for not paying more attention to scientific observations, his perseverance and steadiness were remarkable in view of the pressures and responsibilities he had. At the end, he was simply exhausted, ill, and overwhelmed. In addition to the the Bering **Strait,** the Bering Sea, which is connected with the Arctic Ocean by way of the strait, is named for him.

Chapter Two
Alexander Mackenzie
In the Far Northwest (1789, 1793)

Alexander Mackenzie (c.1764–1820) has been called the most daring of the northwest explorers. A fur trader from Scotland, he traced the course of the 1,100-mile (1,770-kilometer) Mackenzie River in Canada and became the first European to cross the North American continent overland to the Pacific Ocean on his second expedition.

Mackenzie was born near Stornoway on Lewis Island off the northwest coast of Scotland about the year 1764. Ten years later his widowed father took him to New York. But the colonies became embroiled in a revolution with England, so his father sent the boy to Montreal, Canada, for safety and joined the war on the British side. Mackenzie's father died of illness while in the army and the son stayed in school in Montreal.

In about 1779, Mackenzie became a clerk in the fur-trading company of Gregory and McLeod. Five years later, he got his first trading duties—delivering supplies to the company post in Detroit. Not long after, he was made a partner and took up duties at Grand Portage, a post at the end of Lake Superior that linked the region to the interior of Canada. At the company's annual meeting in Grand Portage in 1785, it was decided that Mackenzie would be in charge of the area around

A portrait of Alexander Mackenzie (1764–1820)

the Churchill River in what is now northern Saskatchewan Province in Canada. The headquarters were established at Ile-à-la-Crosse.

This new post put Mackenzie's group in **competition** with the much larger North West Company, a rival of the Hudson's Bay Company. The competition resulted in some violence until the two companies **merged** in 1787. The following year, Mackenzie was happy to accept the job of running North West's post at Lake Athabasca in what are now the Canadian provinces of Alberta and Saskatchewan. He took his cousin Roderick with him for the day-to-day fur-trading business at Fort Chipewyan. This left Mackenzie free to realize his long-held desire to explore.

The first expedition

At the new post, Mackenzie came in contact with American explorer and fur trader Peter Pond. Familiar with the area, Pond had developed a theory. Back in 1776, Captain James Cook of the British navy had described a river that flowed into the Alaskan bay now known as Cook's **Inlet.** Pond believed that the river flowing northwest out of Great Slave Lake, which was northwest of Athabasca, was the one Cook had described. If so, this might be the long-sought Northwest Passage to the Pacific.

Pond retired from exploring in 1788, leaving Mackenzie to test his theory. With the trading post operating smoothly, Mackenzie spent the winter and spring preparing for the journey. On June 3, 1789, he left Fort Chipewyan on Lake Athabasca with four Canadians and two of their wives, one German adventurer,

The Mackenzie River system travels 2,635 miles (4,241 kilometers) through Canada, before emptying into the Beaufort Sea in the Arctic Ocean.

Mackenzie caught sight of the Rocky Mountains twice in his travels.

grew more and more optimistic. Surely, the river was flowing to the Pacific. Surely, this was the Northwest Passage. Mackenzie was more delighted when, on the morning of July 2, 1789, out of the fog he could see the snow-capped Rocky Mountains in the distance, a majestic and welcome sight.

But it did not last long. Instead of the river flowing through the mountains, as Mackenzie had expected if it emptied into the Pacific, it now turned north-ward. After a few days, the explorer had to acknowledge that the river was flowing to the Arctic. However, he decided to follow its course and eventually met Native Americans who told him of dangers ahead if he persisted in traveling the river. Mackenzie was also warned that the journey would take him many winters and he would be an old man before he returned.

Actually, Mackenzie and his group entered the 100-mile (160-kilometer) long delta of the Mackenzie River on July 10, having grown only a few days older. When he took a latitude reading, Mackenzie was surprised to discover how far north he was. He was also disappointed since it confirmed again that this was not the Northwest Passage. And as majestic as the Mackenzie River might be, it was of little use to fur traders.

Mackenzie and his crew stayed four days on an island in the Beaufort Sea. Then they turned homeward before the winter settled in. On the return trip, Mackenzie was already planning his second expedi-

and a Chipewyan named English Chief and his extended family. They traveled up the Peace River to the Slave River to Great Slave Lake. The river was so full of rapids and the lake still so icy that they did not reach its northern shore until June 23. After that, it took another six days to find the river that Pond had described and would eventually be named for Mackenzie.

Once on the river, traveling became easier and sometimes the party went as far as 75 miles in a day. Since the river ran west and sometimes southwest for 300 miles (483 kilometers), Mackenzie

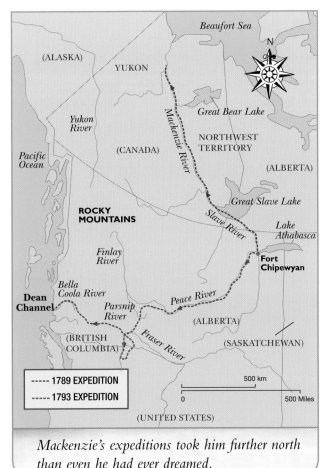

Mackenzie's expeditions took him further north than even he had ever dreamed.

tion. At one point, he even thought about trying for the Pacific Ocean right then, but was discouraged when some Native Americans he met refused to guide him to what they described as the "White Man's Lake." That was probably good fortune for Mackenzie since he arrived back at Fort Chipewyan just two days after the first snowstorm, on September 12, 1789.

Although he had traveled about 3,000 miles (4,828 kilometers) in a little more than 3 months and had mapped one of the world's great rivers, Mackenzie was

disappointed. And that is just what he named the river he had explored—Disappointment. The name was later changed to honor him.

The second expedition

During the winter of his return from the Arctic, Mackenzie went to London to learn more about surveying and navigation. He also studied astronomy and geography, returning to the northwest with a good supply of measuring instruments.

The second expedition left Fort Chipewyan on October 10, 1792. In the party was his second in command, Alexander Mackay, as well as six French-Canadians, and several Native American interpreters. Also included were 3,000 pounds (1,360 kilograms) of supplies and an extremely large and lightweight canoe that Mackenzie had designed. The group spent the winter in a fort they constructed about 200 miles (322 kilometers) up the Peace River, ready for an early start in the spring. On May 9, 1793, they were set to move.

By May 17, Mackenzie again saw the Rocky Mountains. After that, they came to Peace River canyon, a tortuous run of about 22 miles (35 kilometers) full of falls and rapids between rocky cliffs. It took them 6 days to go 9 miles (14 kilometers). Near the end of the month they came to a fork in the river in northeastern British Columbia. There, the Finlay and Parsnip Rivers flowed together into the Peace.

Mackenzie's expedition was slowed by the difficult terrain in Peace River Canyon, British Columbia.

A Native American told Mackenzie that the Parsnip River, although it flowed southeast, would lead him across the mountains to another river that went to the ocean. But for most of June, Mackenzie was certain that he had been given the wrong advice. With mountains surrounding them and constantly plagued by mosquitos and the heat, Mackenzie grew gradually more certain that the Parsnip was not leading them to the sea. But they continued to travel to the Continental Divide and then crossed to the Fraser River (named for Simon Fraser who would travel it to its mouth some time later). But local Native Americans warned them that the river canyon was impassable.

By now Mackenzie had figured out that the only way to the Pacific was overland, not by water. But that would mean back-tracking up the Fraser. To his surprise his weary men agreed. On July 4, wearing backpacks, Mackenzie and his party left the junction of the Fraser and Blackwater rivers heading west.

They walked for fifteen days. New sights greeted them—Native American houses covered with paintings, enormous canoes made from cedar logs, gigantic trees, and a population that existed mainly on salmon rather than meat. On July 17, they reached the Bella Coola River where the friendly local tribes lived in houses built on stilts. Mackenzie was sure he was close to the sea.

And so he was. They continued on the Bella Coola and two days later arrived at the mouth of the river, which emptied into the Dean **Channel** in what is now British

Columbia. Had Mackenzie been a month earlier, he would have run into explorer and navigator George Vancouver, who had arrived at this spot by sea.

Mackenzie had found the Pacific Ocean, becoming the first European to cross the North American continent overland north of Mexico. However, the area Native Americans were pointedly unfriendly, so Mackenzie had to search for two days to find a spot where he could establish his longitude and latitude. On the morning of June 22, he found a large rock ledge in Dean Channel and with a mixture of dye and melted grease, he painted this inscription: "Alexander Mackenzie from Canada by land 22d July 1793." Today, those words have been chiseled into the rock and are preserved in a park.

The later years

Mackenzie had spent ten weeks on the journey west; it took only four weeks to get home. He stayed at Fort Chipewyan during the winter of 1794 and then headed for Montreal. For years, he fought for his idea of having the two largest fur-trading companies, Hudson's Bay and North West, unite and then cooperate with the East India company to open a new trade route to the East. The idea never materialized. Mackenzie became director of a trading company in Montreal and returned to England in 1799. His journal was published in 1801, which was the first time Europe heard the full story of his accomplishments. He was knighted a year later.

This totem pole was found in Bella Coola, British Columbia.

Sir Alexander returned to Canada in 1802 and joined the colonial legislature in 1804, going back to London the following year. Finally, he retired to Scotland at the age of 48. He died in Edinburgh in 1820.

Alexander Mackenzie was a great leader who undertook two of the most difficult explorations in North America. His determination and stamina pulled him through times of great danger and discouragement. He explored a major North American river and followed his dream to the Pacific Ocean.

Chapter Three
George Vancouver
Mapping the Coast (1791–1794)

Explorer by explorer, year by year, Americans were learning more about the incredibly huge land that stretched westward from the Mississippi River. One who contributed a great deal to that knowledge was an English navigator named George Vancouver (1757–1798). With great precision and under great difficulty, he surveyed the Pacific coast from the area of San Francisco north to present-day British Columbia. Vancouver Island off British Columbia as well as cities in that province and in the state of Washington on the Columbia River are named for him. In large part, Vancouver put an end to speculations of a Northwest Passage to the Far East. He showed that there was no continuous body of water between the Pacific Ocean and Hudson Bay in northeast Canada. The thoroughness and accuracy of his mapping expedition is still impressive centuries later.

To sea with Captain Cook

Vancouver was born to an Anglo-Dutch family in King's Lynn, Norfolk, England, on June 22, 1757. It is believed that the family name was originally van Couverden. George was the youngest of five children of Bridget and John Jasper Vancouver. His father was an official in the customs office.

A portrait of George Vancouver (1757–1798)

King's Lynn was an ancient English port, and young George grew up with the smell of the sea in his nostrils. Although there are no records to prove it, he and his two brothers, John and Charles, were probably educated at the Lynn Grammar School, which was already ancient in his day. His mother died when he was eleven, and at the age of thirteen, he joined the Royal Navy as a midshipman candidate. His family's connections got him an appointment to serve with English navigator James Cook. In the early 1770s, Lieutenant

Cook was already famous. All told, Cook (1728–1779) made three expeditions to the Pacific Ocean. His voyages made more peacefully accomplished changes to the map of the world than any other single person in history.

From 1772–1775, Vancouver accompanied Cook on his second expedition. They left Plymouth **Sound,** England, on July 13, 1772 in the *Resolution,* 462 tons, accompanied by the *Adventure,* 336 tons.

A painting depicts James Cook, who lived from 1728–1779.

It must have been an exciting adventure for a 15-year-old. The expedition ranks as one of the greatest of all sailing voyages, in search of a huge southern continent that was thought to exist. On this voyage, Cook visited Tahiti, New Hebrides, New Caledonia, and he skirted Antarctica. It is said that as the *Resolution* neared the southern continent, young Vancouver hung off the prow (the front) of the ship so that he could claim—for quite some time—that he had been farther south than any other person. It was not until 1820 that the continent of Antarctica was actually sighted; Russian Fabian Gottlieb von Bellingshausen, Englishman Edward Bransfield, and American Nathaniel Palmer all claimed to be the first.

Perhaps the greatest of feats on Cook's second voyage, as on the first, was that not one sailor died of the dietary disease known as **scurvy.** Cook insisted that his crew include sauerkraut and an extract made from oranges in their diet. When he returned to England from this voyage, he was given the prestigious Copley Medal for the paper he prepared on scurvy. He was also promoted to captain.

Vancouver also sailed with Cook on this third and last voyage (1776–1779) to the Pacific. This time he was a midshipman aboard the *Discovery.* This expedition was looking for a northwest passage around Canada and Alaska or a northeast passage around Siberia. Unfortunately, at a stopover in Hawaii, Cook was killed on the beach when a dispute erupted on February 14, 1779, with Native Polynesians over the theft of a small boat. Vancouver was one of the crew who rowed ashore to recover Cook's body. The *Discovery* returned to England in October 1780 and Vancouver was promoted to lieutenant.

Over the next nine years, Vancouver served in the North Sea and the Caribbean on various assignments for England, including a sea battle in the West Indies in 1782. In 1789, he retired from active duty. However, the following year, now with the rank of commander, he was assigned as second in command on another expedition to the South Pacific. However, about this time Spain and England signed the Nootka Convention in which Spain gave up its claims to the northwestern coast of North America. That included several British ships that had been taken by the Spanish off what is now Vancouver Island in British Columbia. Instead of the South Pacific expedition, Vancouver was put in command of a voyage to the Pacific Northwest to take possession of the ships and to make a **survey** of the western coast. It would be his major accomplishment.

The great survey

On April 1, 1791, Vancouver left England in the *Discovery* accompanied by the smaller *Chatham*. He sailed

A sketch of Cook's ship Discovery

around the Cape of Good Hope in South Africa, crossed the Indian Ocean to Australia, moved on to New Zealand, and reached Tahiti in late December. From there, he headed toward Hawaii just in time for a war going on in the islands. It resulted in the unification of all of the Hawaiian islands under King Kamehameha. Now, Vancouver set his compass for the western coast of North America. He arrived about 100 miles (160 kilometers) north of San Francisco Bay on April 18, 1792, a little more than a year after he had left England. He was ready to chart the western coast.

At first, the work was relatively easy. The coastline stretching from present-day San Francisco to the state of Washington is, for the most part, unbroken. Vancouver had the crew take endless compass bearings, depth soundings, and numerous astronomical observations. When he reached Cape

Disappointment, he noticed a large discharge of water into the sea. However, he did not stop to investigate. If he had, he would have become the first European to see the Columbia River, part of the boundary between present-day Oregon and Washington. Only two days later, Vancouver encountered the American Robert Gray in his ship the *Columbia*. Gray announced he had only the day before sited the river that he named for his vessel.

On May 1, 1792, Vancouver and his crew rounded Cape Flattery and entered the **Strait** of Juan de Fuca, which separates Vancouver Island from the mainland of Canada. Here, surveying became really hard work. The two ships had entered a bewildering tangle of **sounds, channels, inlets,** islands, and **coves.** It was much too dangerous for the ships to maneuver, so most of the surveying work had to be done in small boats.

Vancouver found suitable mooring for the *Discovery* and the *Chatham* and set up an observation camp on shore. The exact site of this camp is unknown. Thus began a boring schedule that went on for three summer seasons. Under the command of Vancouver or one of his lieutenants, the small boats would go out for ten days or more. They carried provisions, equipment, and arms in case they ran into unfriendly native peoples.

Although Vancouver was respected by his crew, he was not well liked. His command was ruthless, even cruel, in the way he drove the men. Conditions were

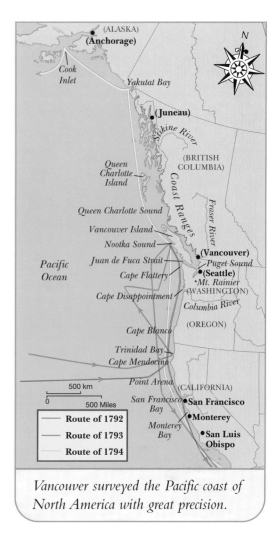

Vancouver surveyed the Pacific coast of North America with great precision.

less than ideal. While the officers slept in tents, the crew had little shelter from the almost constant rain. In addition, Vancouver was a dangerously moody man, his spells shifting from wild fury to an almost trancelike state. He would erupt into a tantrum at the slightest infraction, leaving his subordinates to stare at him in awe and fear. During the winter months, which were spent in the Hawaiian Islands, Vancouver would

Mt. Rainier is 14,410 feet (4,392 meters) tall, making it the tallest mountain in the state of Washington.

often restrict the men to their ships or order more **surveys.** These behavioral swings were all said to be symptoms of the illness that would later cause his death.

Yet, despite the horrific conditions, Vancouver and his crew did remarkable work. Over the three seasons, 10,000 miles (16,093 kilometers) were covered in the small boats, more than 1,700 miles (2,736 kilometers) of shoreline mapped out in intricate detail. Over one 23-day period, they mapped 60 miles (96 kilometers) of coastline by rowing over 800 miles (1,287 kilometers).

All in all over the three-year period, Vancouver surveyed the complex waterways of Puget **Sound,** named for one of his ship's officers; sited and named Mt.

Rainier, for an officer he had served with in the West Indies; and claimed possession of the Pacific Northwest for England, calling it New Georgia for King George III. At one point, Vancouver's ship ran aground in the fog off the northern end of Vancouver Island. The next morning at high tide, the ship drifted off the sandbar and entered Queen Charlotte's **Sound.** This proved Vancouver Island was indeed just that —an island.

In August of 1792, Vancouver tried to complete his other mission. He sailed into Nootka Sound to take possession of the British ships and the Spanish settlement as per the treaty. But he ran into some trouble. Although Vancouver and the Spanish commander, Don Francisco de la Bodega y Quadra, were friendly enough, they could not quite agree on how the takeover should be carried out. Finally, the two captains proposed that, to be fair, they should name the island Quadra and Vancouver Island. The name stuck until the mid-1800s. A smaller island in the **Strait** of Georgia is now known as Quadra. The dispute over taking possession of the area was later settled in Europe.

During 1793, Vancouver charted the coastline as far south as San Luis Obispo, California. At one point he stopped at the entrance to the Columbia River, which he had missed on his way north. But the *Discovery* could not cross the **sandbars,** so Vancouver sent Lieutenant William Broughton upriver in the smaller *Chatham*. Broughton got as far as 100 miles (160 kilometers) upstream to what is now Vancouver, Washington, where the Willamette River flows into the Columbia. He also saw and named Mt. Hood for a British admiral. Then, in the usual grand manner of the times, Broughton claimed the entire area for the British king. Later, Great Britain tried to claim ownership by reasoning that its ship had found where the river began and Gray had not. The United States merely said that Gray had gotten there first, a fact that settled the later dispute over the boundary of Oregon.

Historians have long wondered how so meticulous a man as Vancouver could have missed the Columbia River. He noted nothing about it in his official journal. Perhaps it was just Vancouver's overall feelings about rivers, which he seemed to regard as insignificant. He had been ordered not to go exploring in places that might mean an unnecessary loss of time. That might have been how he regarded the Columbia.

Early in 1794, Vancouver returned to Hawaii and saw King Kamehameha. Apparently the king proposed giving his nation to Great Britain. Although Vancouver accepted the unusual offer, the British government never did.

Vancouver Island is the largest island on the Pacific coast of North America.

Vancouver left Hawaii early in the year, sailing north to Alaska. Over the next few months, he charted Cook **Inlet** off southern Alaska, the site of present-day Anchorage. In August, the long, intensive, and backbreaking **survey** was complete. Appropriately, Vancouver named his last stop off the Alaska-British Columbia border "Port Conclusion." It is said that the weary crew and an increasingly ill captain celebrated the event with a "double allowance of grog."

Going home

His work done, Vancouver headed for England. The ships sailed southward, making some final surveys of the coast north of San Francisco. On the long journey home, Vancouver kept checking and rechecking his charts and maps

Alaska's Cook Inlet ranges from 80 to 9 miles (129 to 14 kilometers) wide.

to be sure of their accuracy. At one point, he stopped at Cape San Lucas at the southern extreme of Baja California. He knew that the position of San Lucas had been reliably plotted in 1769. So, he checked his own findings for the site against that position and discovered he was within one mile of accuracy. Understandably pleased with himself, Vancouver checked and rechecked everything again at sea.

The homeward voyage took the *Discovery* around Cape Horn at the tip of South America and into the Atlantic Ocean. As he neared Europe, he joined a British convoy, which was out patrolling the waters because Britain and France were once again at war with one another. On September 12, 1795, Vancouver sighted the coast of Ireland and three days later reached England after nearly five years at sea.

Vancouver was pleased to learn that during his long absence he had been promoted to captain. He was not so pleased, however, to spend a good deal of the next two years fighting to get his back pay from the Admiralty Board. The rest of his time was spent writing a journal of the expedition. It was published along with maps and illustrations in 1798, entitled *A Voyage of Discovery to the North Pacific Ocean and Round the World in the Years 1790–1795*.

Captain Vancouver retired to the village of Petersham, north of London. One of his officers, Thomas Pitt, Lord Camelford, accused him publicly of unfair treatment and challenged him to a duel. Vancouver refused. Later, the two met on a London street and Camelford beat Vancouver with his cane.

From all accounts and for whatever reasons, it could not have been easy to sail with George Vancouver. He was a hard and perhaps even cruel man, although there are no accounts of his working his crews any harder than he worked himself. But if it was not easy to sail with him, at least it was relatively safe by the standards of the time. During nearly five years at sea covering more than 70,000 nautical miles, he lost only six men out of a total crew of 146. That was well below the standard losses of the day for even a much shorter voyage. In addition, at the time when deaths from **scurvy** were the norm, he had but one incidence of the condition on the voyage and that was because a cook disobeyed his orders. He demonstrated that scurvy did not have to be a factor on long sea voyages.

Cape San Lucas was one of the stops that Vancouver made on his trip back to Europe.

The great navigator died in Petersham on May 10, 1798, a few months before his book was published. Some authorities think he had long been suffering from Graves disease, a disorder stemming from too much thyroid hormone. This condition can cause all sorts of physical problems as well as severe mood swings and bouts of anger and listlessness. However, some historians doubt he was ill and think Vancouver was just overworked and overtired.

Vancouver, who never married, spent his final days bedridden and in the care of his brother. He completed the last few pages of his journal just before he died. Although he never lived to hear the praise for a job well done, he probably would not have been surprised. His charts were remarkably accurate. A tireless, demanding leader, George Vancouver was a brilliant navigator who left his mark forever on northwestern North America.

Chapter Four

Robert Gray
A Claim on Oregon (1792)

The earliest explorers to the Americas were Europeans. As the years passed, adventurers who were born in Canada or the United States began to travel around, too. One of them was a sea captain named Robert Gray (1755–1806). Not only was he the first American to sail around the globe, but his was the first ship to enter the mighty Columbia River on the boundary between present-day Oregon and Washington. In so doing, he gave the United States a vitally important claim to the Oregon Territory.

Around the world

Robert Gray was born in Tiverton, Rhode Island, on May 10, 1755. His great-grandfather was probably Edward Gray, who had settled in Plymouth, Massachusetts, in 1643 and married a niece of Edward Winslow, governor of the colony. Like many young men of his time, Gray looked to the sea for his career. He served in the Continental Navy during the American Revolution and after the war he joined a Massachusetts trading company.

In September 1787, commanding the little **sloop** *Lady Washington,* Gray left Boston with Captain John Kendrick, a veteran merchant sailor. Kendrick was commanding the full-rigged *Columbia Rediviva,* generally just known as the *Columbia.* It had three masts and was

A portrait of Robert Gray (1755–1806)

about 212 tons (192 metric tons). The ships set out on the first U.S. trading voyage to China. Six Boston businessmen had the idea of linking the fast-growing fur trade of the Pacific Northwest to the old but profitable commerce of the Far East. Gray and Kendrick were sent to trade with the native peoples of the Pacific Northwest for sea-otter **pelts,** then take the fur cargo to China and trade it for tea. The promoters hoped that the tea would be sold for a profit in Boston.

Although the two ships left Boston together, they were separated in a heavy storm while sailing around Cape Horn at the tip of South America. Gray landed on the shore of present-day Oregon. The crew needed water and berries because many of them were suffering from **scurvy.** With the addition of fruits, fresh fish, greens, and deer meat given to them by the Native Americans, the crew members soon recovered. Most of Gray's dealings with native peoples on his voyages were peaceful, although there were a few instances of hostility against the fur traders.

Gray resumed sail, going north to Nootka, off Vancouver Island, which was the center of the sea-otter trade. There he was reunited with Kendrick. Nearly a year had passed since the expedition left Boston. After building huts on the shore, everyone settled down to wait out the winter.

At last spring came to the Northwest and Gray in the smaller ship energetically began to trade for the precious sea otter pelts. But he soon became distressed by Kendrick's lack of drive and leadership, which caused him to lose the crew's confidence. Although

Columbia *and* Lady Washington *were separated by a storm while sailing around Cape Horn, on the tip of South America.*

Heavily-wooded Vancouver Island is separated from the United States by Juan de Fuca Strait.

mile (67,592-kilometer) voyage brought great prestige to the young country and opened up new possibilities for trade.

Exploring the northwest

The *Columbia* was refitted and on one fine morning in September 1790, Gray, after only one month ashore, departed Boston once again. This time he was headed once more for what would later be called Vancouver Island in the Pacific Northwest. The *Columbia* carried a cargo of trading goods valued at more than $25,000. It included 135 barrels of beef, 60 barrels of pork, 1,500 pounds (680 kilograms) of gunpowder, 2,000 bricks, New England and West Indian rum, and a lot of tea, sugar, chocolate, and other items such as copper and blankets for trade with the native peoples. Not only was Gray in command of the expedition to explore the Northwest, but he was also part owner in the venture. In addition he carried a letter signed by President George Washington and Secretary of State Thomas Jefferson. It said that he should not trade in any Spanish-held territory nor enter any Spanish-held ports. Nootka, where Gray had traded earlier, was now involved in a dispute between Spain and England, so that profitable site was off the list. The *Columbia* passed the Cape Verde Islands off the western coast of Africa and turned east, stopping for several days at the Falkland Islands near Cape Horn.

Kendrick had been designated as the commander of the voyage, he transferred his authority to Gray, who took command of the *Columbia*.

On July 30, Gray left Vancouver and sailed to China. There he traded the sea-otter **pelts** for a cargo of tea. The mission was nearly complete, except that Gray, being new to the trading business, did not secure a profitable return in the trading exchange. Nonetheless, he began the return voyage in late July 1789.

Gray sailed into Boston harbor on August 10, 1790, to be greeted with a 13-gun salute. It was not the success of the venture—it just about broke even—that brought such a great response. Gray had become the first American to sail around the globe. It was the first time that the American flag had been seen in many corners of the world. Gray's 42,000-

Gray arrived at Vancouver Island in the South Atlantic in June 1791. There he once again met Kendrick, who was heading for China on the *Lady Washington* with a load of furs. Kendrick's story has a bizarre ending. After sailing for China that September, he apparently sold the ship to himself and seemingly never intended to return to Boston. Sometime later while at anchor in Hawaii, he was killed when an English ship fired a "friendly" salute that was accidentally loaded with a cannonball. His ship was later wrecked in Southeast Asia.

Gray sailed up the coast as far north as southern Alaska and as far south as present-day Oregon looking for likely trading sites. As winter approached, he decided to anchor at Clayoquot **Sound,** not far from Nootka and near the village of what is now Tofino. Gray and the nearly 50 men under his command built a long house near the edge of the water, naming it Fort Defiance. They manned the fort with muskets and cannon in case of attack from hostile Native Americans and spent the winter months building the *Adventure,* a 45-ton trading sloop.

In the spring of 1792, Gray sent the *Adventure* to the north under the command of first mate Robert Haswell. He sailed south in the *Columbia.* As more and more traders heard of the lucrative northwestern coast, it was becoming more and more difficult to find worthwhile trading spots. Gray reasoned that if he could find a new or unexplored river or sound, he might encounter native peoples who were not used to fur traders. Therefore, they might accept lower prices for their furs.

In early spring while on his quest for the unexplored, Gray arrived at the mouth of what was known as the River of the West. Gray had heard of it. Jonathan Carver, explorer and author of adventure books, had written of its existence, calling it "River Oregan." The Spaniard Bruno de Hezeta had several years earlier apparently seen the mouth and his siting

Gray spent the winter of 1791–1792 at Clayoquot Sound.

The Columbia River is the largest North American river to flow into the Pacific Ocean.

was noted on some Spanish maps. But no one—including George Vancouver—had sailed into the river.

Now, Gray thought he had found the so-called River of the West. But he also found dangerous currents and sweeping **sandbars** that prevented him from entering the mouth. So, Gray sailed north where he chose a spot to drop anchor and think about what to do.

It was at this point that Gray met George Vancouver who was surveying the Pacific coast. Gray, who was known to be something of a chatterbox, could not resist telling Vancouver of what he thought he had found. Vancouver was not much interested at the time and only later on a return voyage entered the river that Gray had by then claimed.

Gray continued north and sailed into the harbor that now bears his name where the modern-day Washington ports

of Hoquiam and Aberdeen are located. Then, he seems to have made up his mind about the river, for he turned south again. In early spring, he arrived at the mouth of the river. Once again he could see that entering it would not be easy. Foaming water churned dangerously over the sandbars. But this time Gray sent ahead a small boat to guide him. Following the smaller vessel, he brought his ship safely through the bars and entered the freshwater of the river that he named for his ship, the *Columbia*.

Gray sailed up the Columbia for about 25 miles (40 kilometers). He traded with the local native peoples for about 10 days, but since the trading was not as good as he had hoped, he sailed back downstream and headed for home. That was the only time he saw what turned out to be his great discovery.

The later years

His ship once again loaded with **pelts,** Gray met up with the *Adventure*. First mate Haswell came back on board the *Columbia* and the *Adventure* was later sold

Sea otters were very valuable in the fur trade of the late 1700s.

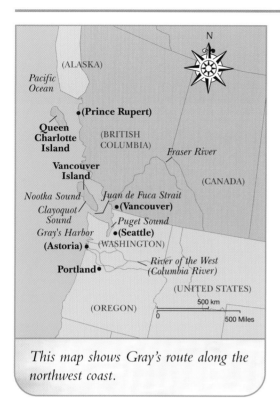

This map shows Gray's route along the northwest coast.

to the Spanish. Gray sailed to China for the second time. On July 20, 1793, he returned to Boston, anchoring at Long Wharf to a salute of eleven guns. He had circled the globe twice.

Gray was right about the increasing difficulty in making money in the fur trade, although it would continue to be quite profitable until about 1805. Between 1801–1802, for example, a total of 15,000 sea-otter skins were collected by the fifteen ships from all countries operating in the area. After that high, however, a sea-otter skin that had brought about $120 in China had dropped to $20. After the Americans entered the trade in the late 1780s, they soon drove the British from the field. By 1800 the city of Boston had a near monopoly on trade in the north Pacific. When sea otters became scarce, the search moved down the California coast.

Gray's ship *Columbia* was demolished by the United States in 1801. The cancellation date in the U.S. National Archives says, "October 15" and the inscription says, "ript to pieces." It is unknown what happened to the *Adventure*.

The second voyage was Gray's last around the world. In 1794, at the age of 39, he married Martha Atkins and settled down to a life with his family and sailing the Atlantic coast out of Boston. They had five children. During the summer of 1806, he was on a trip to Charlestown, South Carolina, where he became ill, presumably of yellow fever. It is believed that Robert Gray was buried at sea.

Explorer, navigator, and trader Robert Gray never knew the importance of his trip up the Columbia River that day in May 1792. Before his travels, the Pacific Northwest was largely fought over by Spain and Great Britain. But his voyage followed by the overland **trek** to the Columbia by Lewis and Clark gave the young United States a strong claim to the territory. Strangely, the British accepted Gray's name for the river and called that region of the Pacific Northwest "Columbia District." But it is now called "Oregon," supposedly from the Plains Indians. Eventually, Gray's work led to the creation of the Oregon Territory in 1848 and later to the states of Washington, Oregon, and Idaho.

Chapter Five

Meriwether Lewis and William Clark
The Great Overland Expedition (1804–1806)

Their names go together like salt and pepper or Antony and Cleopatra. No one says "Lewis and Clark, the explorers." That is because, together, they are America's most famous explorers, a team that led the first official U.S. expedition across North America to the Pacific Ocean and back. Stories and plays and television dramas have been written about them. They are among America's earliest heroes.

Lewis and Clark were wonderful complements to each other. Although he tended to be quiet and reserved, Lewis was the more educated of the two and was better trained for the expedition. Clark was by nature more outgoing and warm and was by far the better natural woodsman. The two men worked together so well and in so meticulous a manner that they brought back from their journey a remarkable set of diaries and maps. Their journals not only opened the American Northwest to settlers and more exploration, but they also helped to erase fear and ignorance about the region. Lewis and Clark also dispelled the notion that there was an easy way to cross America by water.

The two men had much in common besides their famous trip. Both were born in Virginia and both in August. Lewis was born in Albermarle County on

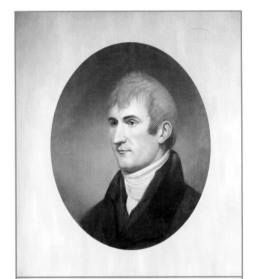

Top, Meriwether Lewis (1774–1809)

Bottom, William Clark (1770–1838)

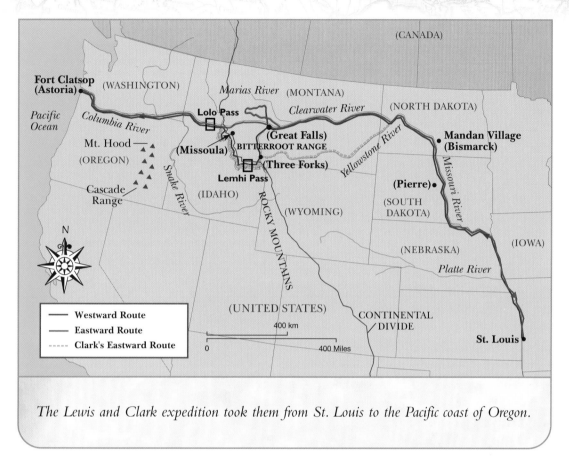

The Lewis and Clark expedition took them from St. Louis to the Pacific coast of Oregon.

August 18, 1774, and Clark in Caroline County on August 1, 1770. Both served in the military and both later became governors. Lewis died under mysterious circumstances in Nashville, Tennessee in 1809; Clark outlived him by 29 years. He died at home in St. Louis, Missouri, in 1838.

Early years for Lewis

Lewis grew up on a farm not far from Charlottesville. Meriwether became the man of his family at the age of five when his father died in the American Revolution. With his mother, he helped to take care of his younger brother. He became an expert hunter and developed a love of the wilderness.

Lewis went to school until he was eighteen years old and thought he would spend his future on the farm. However, he was also an officer in the local **militia.** When President George Washington called for militia volunteers to end the Whiskey Rebellion, Lewis answered.

In western Pennsylvania, farmers opposed a tax on liquor by staging a rebellion in 1794. They attacked federal revenue officers who tried to collect the tax. Washington ordered some 13,000 troops into the area, but there was no fight because the farmers backed down. Two of the rebels were convicted of treason, although the president later pardoned them. The Whiskey Rebellion was important in history because it was the first time the young U.S. government asserted its authority to move military forces within state boundaries.

Although he saw little action in Pennsylvania, Lewis found that he liked the military. He wrote to his mother, "I am quite delighted with a soldier's life." Deciding to make it a career, he joined the regular army and became a captain in the First Infantry under General Anthony Wayne. He took part in wars against Native Americans in what was called the "Old Northwest Territory." It was there that he first met William Clark, who was commanding a special company

A federal revenue officer is attacked during the Whiskey Rebellion of 1794.

of sharpshooters. The two men liked each other immediately.

Thomas Jefferson was inaugurated as the third president of the United States in 1801. He asked Lewis to become his personal secretary. This is equivalent to today's White House Chief of Staff. Lewis held the post for two years.

Early years for Clark

John and Ann Rogers Clark moved from Albemarle to Caroline County about 30 miles (48 kilometers) north of Richmond 15 years before their ninth child William was born. He had red hair, which was significant in the Clark family. According to tradition, a child who inherited red hair would become a person of vitality and force. Clark's brother, George Rogers, another redhead, was a famous general in the American Revolution.

William Clark received little formal education on his family's plantation. That was not unusual for the time and place. A later historian called him "a creative speller." He also had an interesting way of capitalizing words for no apparent reason in the middle of a sentence. However, Clark developed a love of the outdoors and some knowledge of business and government affairs from visitors to his home. He learned to ride and hunt, to observe nature, to make maps, and to **survey** the land. Clark was taught the manners of a Virginia gentleman, yet always retained something of the frontier in his speech and actions.

Clark fought in the Battle of Fallen Timbers, 1794.

The Clark family was much affected by the American Revolution. The oldest son, John, a major, was taken prisoner by the British at Germantown and died in 1783. Occasionally, the family would get news of the deeds and whereabouts of George Rogers.

Clark and his family left Virginia in late 1784 for the western frontier land of Kentucky. By early spring they were floating down the Ohio River on a flatboat that carried their furniture, slaves, animals, and equipment for a new home.

They were met at Louisville by Clark's brother, now a general. The family settled into their new home, Mulberry Hill, outside of town. It is there that young Clark grew up. Even after his parents died in 1799, he continued to call Mulberry Hill his home.

Clark may have joined his brother in **campaigns** against Native Americans in the early 1780s, as white settlers were encroaching deeper into Indian territory. In 1791, General Arthur St. Clair was caught in a surprise attack and lost 600 men. This left the western frontier defenseless to attack. After that, Clark applied to the army to enter regular service. He was commissioned on March 7, 1792, as lieutenant of infantry.

For four years Clark served with General Anthony Wayne and fought in Cincinnati and against the Chickasaw near Memphis. He was also with Wayne in the Battle of Fallen Timbers on August 20, 1794. This decisive victory over the Northwest Indian Confederation ended decades of warfare and opened the way to permanent white settlement, mainly in Ohio. It was at this time that Clark met and became friends with Meriwether Lewis. The meeting would soon change his life.

For some time before Fallen Timbers, Clark had been losing interest in the military. But the army urged him to remain, so he did not retire until July 1, 1796, when he returned to Mulberry Hill ready for a more quiet life. It might have been quiet, but it was busy. His brother George Rogers had lost a good deal of his money during his years in service, and Clark made many trips to Virginia, New Orleans, and the new capital, Washington, to try to secure his brother's funds from the state of Virginia.

Then, in 1803, William Clark received a letter from his friend Meriwether Lewis. He was about to set off on a fantastic adventure.

Thomas Jefferson and the great Northwest

Thomas Jefferson was the third president of the United States (1801–1809). He was a lawyer, farmer, inventor, botanist, architect, writer, and scientist, among other things. He also loved information and, in April 1803, when France sold 828,000 square miles (2,144,510 square kilometers) of largely unmapped North American territory to the United States, Jefferson wanted to know more. He wanted to find out about the land he had bought for $15 million, or about three cents an acre.

What Jefferson did know was that the Louisiana Purchase, as it was called, had just about doubled the size of the United States. That made it one of the greatest land deals in history. Napoleon Bonaparte, leader of France, sold the Louisiana Territory to the United States at such a bargain price for two reasons. France was short of money. And Napoleon was afraid that his old enemy, Great Britain, was about to capture the French-held territory in America, especially the port of New Orleans. Wary about fighting a war so far from home,

Thomas Jefferson sent Lewis and Clark on their mission of exploration.

Napoleon decided it was better to sell the land than lose it to the British.

Now that the United States had the land, it had to decide what to do with it. At the beginning of the 1800s, most Americans lived east of the Appalachian Mountains. They traveled on roads that went from poor to terrible. West of the mountains there were no roads at all. Nobody went faster than the speed of a horse anyway. It took three days to travel by land from Boston to New York City, and that was only a distance of 175 miles (282 kilometers). The country was just 20 years old at the time of the Louisiana Purchase. Most of its leaders were worried about holding the 17 states together, not about the land beyond the mountains, which most people could not get to anyway.

But Jefferson thought a lot about that territory beyond the mountains. He decided that information about its natural resources and cultures could only help the young United States to grow. So, the president convinced the Congress, which especially in the early years was exceedingly stingy with money, to allow $2,500 for the entire expedition. And he chose his personal secretary, Meriwether Lewis, to lead it.

Although Jefferson had great confidence in his young friend, Lewis was not really trained for an expedition of such magnitude. But Jefferson realized that it would be almost impossible to find someone of intelligence and honest character who was also an expert woodsman and a trained scientist and knew something about the culture of Native Americans. Lewis excelled in all those qualities except the trained scientist part. So, Jefferson sent the young man to Philadelphia to work and learn with the leading scientists of the day at the American Philosophical Society, which Lewis did from January 1 until March 15, 1803.

"The object of your mission," said Jefferson, "is to explore the Missouri River and such principal streams of it, as by its course and communication with the waters of the Pacific ocean, whether the Columbia, Oregan, Colorado or any other river may offer the most direct and practicable water communication across the continent for the purposes of commerce." Lewis was also to learn about the Native Americans who lived in this vast territory and to find out all about the animals, climate, soil, and terrain of the region—in short, everything.

The Corps of Discovery

William Clark readily accepted Lewis's invitation to join him as co-leader of the expedition. Lewis received the letter of acceptance in July 1803.

Meriwether Lewis left Philadelphia in July and had hoped to meet Clark at St. Louis in August. But the **keelboat** he was building for the expedition caused much delay. This large, squarish vessel with 22 oars would carry supplies. When it was ready, Lewis floated down the Ohio River and finally met Clark in October. The two men formally shook hands, which signified that the expedition had begun. They spent the next two weeks selecting the rest of their crew.

Congress had authorized the expedition on July 2, 1803, to include 12 men, known as the Corps of Discovery. By the time the **trek** really got started, the number had expanded to 43. Lewis kept coming up with reasons to add to the personnel list. Both Lewis and Clark were very careful about the men they authorized to accompany them on this dangerous trip. Clark especially was an excellent judge of men. Recruiting was fairly easy, however, for there was no lack of volunteers. Word had spread about this unusual—and exciting—venture.

Except for the interpreters, the men selected were hunters, gunsmiths, and carpenters. Most were in the army. They

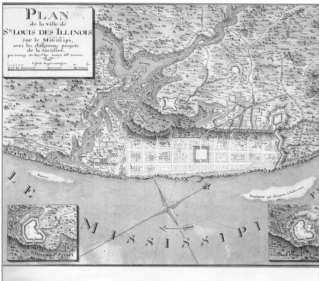

A French map shows St. Louis in the early 1800s.

In addition, they carried items such as beads, needles and thread, and cloth for trade with native peoples. Besides the **keelboat,** the expedition also included three oversized canoes and two large rowboats.

At last in 1803, the great three-year **trek** from St. Louis to the Pacific Ocean and back was underway. It would succeed largely because of the harmonious leadership of its two principal explorers, who were so well suited that what one lacked in a skill or personality trait the other provided.

On the Missouri

Lewis and Clark spent the winter of 1803–1804 at Wood River on the east side of the Mississippi. Clark took charge of training the men. Lewis made frequent trips into St. Louis to talk with fur traders who had traveled to the upper reaches of the Missouri, North America's longest river at 2,714 miles (4,367 kilometers). The land of the Louisiana Purchase was formally transferred to the United States from France on March 10, 1804. Lewis was present at the ceremony in St. Louis.

The great expedition finally pushed off on May 14, 1804. They rowed and sailed up the Mississippi to its junction with the Missouri above St. Louis. Before long, they learned why the Missouri is called mighty and fearsome. It changes course often and is largely frozen in winter. Melting ice adds to melting snow, making the Missouri's flow very power-

were paid $10 a month—Lewis got the army pay raised from the usual $5 monthly for privates—plus the promises of army discharge upon their return and a grant of land in the West. Their best hunter and scout was John Colter, who would in 1807 become the first white man to see what is now Yellowstone National Park. The youngest member was George Shannon, 18 years old, who later became a senator from Kentucky. He was an expert hunter and entertained the others with his fine singing voice. Unfortunately, he also seemed to have a bad sense of direction since he got lost from the others several times during the journey.

Besides the personnel, there were supplies to be carried. These included rifles, gunpowder, candles, clothing, fishhooks, mosquito netting, flour, and salt pork; other meat would come from hunting.

ful. In addition, the Missouri receives large deposits of silt, giving it the nickname Big Muddy. Sometimes there was no wind, sometimes the waters were too strong to row against. Then the men towed the keelboat by ropes as they walked along the riverbanks. There were **sandbars** to maneuver around. And there were the never-ending mosquitoes.

By late July, the party had traveled a little beyond the mouth of the Platte River, where they met members of the Oto tribe. In general, most of their meetings with Native Americans were conducted in a friendly manner, although

An aerial view shows the juncture of the Missouri and Mississippi rivers.

not without incident. The pattern was to give gifts to the Native Americans and inform them that the "great father"—referring to the president of the United States—was a friend upon whom they could depend. Some Native Americans accepted the white man's stated role as leader, others did not. In any case, the promises of eternal friendship made by both sides were not kept.

In August the first death occurred in the Corps of Discovery. Sergeant Charles Floyd, age 22, had been complaining of illness for some days. He died on August 20 and was buried at what was named Floyd's Bluff near present-day Sioux City, Iowa. It is believed his death was from a ruptured appendix. Floyd became the first U.S. soldier to die west of the Mississippi River and the only member of the expedition to die during the three-year journey. More trouble came shortly after Floyd's death, when young Shannon got lost. He turned up 16 days later.

In late September, near present-day Pierre, South Dakota, Lewis and Clark met the Teton Sioux people and had some anxious moments. The Sioux just laughed at their offer of trinkets as a gesture of friendship. Soon warriors armed with bows and arrows were facing army muskets. After some shouting back and forth by Clark and Sioux chief Black Buffalo, tempers cooled and the

A replica of Fort Mandan stands today on the Missouri River near Washburn, North Dakota.

two sides joined in a general celebration. However, Lewis and Clark decided to leave the next day.

By October, the expedition had reached the territory of the Arikara. One of them agreed to accompany the group to the land of the Mandans, where the expedition planned to winter near present-day Bismarck, North Dakota.

The Bird Woman

Lewis and Clark spent the winter of 1804–1805 in a small stockade they called Fort Mandan. They were 1,600 miles (2,575 kilometers) from St. Louis and had averaged about 9 miles (15 kilometers) a day. In the friendly Mandan village, Lewis and Clark met a member of the Shoshone tribe who was to become their most famous guide and interpreter. Her name was Sacajawea (sak-uh-juh-*wee*-uh), which means Bird Woman. So much has been written about her that it is difficult to tell where truth leaves off and legend begins.

Sacajawea was probably about sixteen or seventeen when she joined Lewis and Clark. She had been captured by Mandans years before, who sold her to the French fur trader Toussaint Charbonneau. Lewis and Clark had already hired Charbonneau as a guide when they learned that Sacajawea, one of his two wives, was a Shoshone. They knew that they would soon be crossing Shoshone land and would need help in understanding the language. They asked her and her husband to accompany them, even though she was pregnant. She agreed and seemed to like the military-like life of the expedition. Her baby, a boy she named Pomp, went along, too. Clark often called the lad Pompey, after the great Roman soldier. Many times during the journey, Sacajawea's ability to interpret and sometimes her mere presence with the infant eased the way for peaceful negotiations between the explorers and Native Americans.

Unknown territory

On April 7, 1805, the Corps of Discovery, plus Sacajawea and the baby, set off into unknown territory. No white person had ever traveled farther up the Missouri. That day Lewis wrote in his journal, "I could not but esteem this moment of my departure as among the most happy of my life."

The expedition entered what is now Montana in late April and soon came in contact with what Lewis described in his journal as a "monster"—an awesome grizzly bear. From then on, the group was exceedingly cautious when they saw evidence of one of the "monsters."

By June, they reached the place where "the river splits in two." Their Native American hosts had not mentioned a fork in the river. Which was the real Missouri? Taking some of the men, Lewis traveled the north fork, with Clark to the south. Lewis soon decided that his was not the continuation of the Missouri. He named the river Marias after his cousin Maria Wood, then turned around and caught up with Clark and his group.

Now heading up the main stream in mid-June, the expedition was stopped first by an amazing sound and then by an amazing sight. First, they heard a great continuous roar in the distance. After several more miles, they saw rushing water cascading over waterfalls at a drop of some 92 feet (28 meters). They had reached the main rapids of the Missouri, at present-day Great Falls, Montana.

This statue of Sacajawea is located in Bismarck, North Dakota.

The expedition was temporarily stopped by the rapids at Great Falls, Montana.

Land of Shoshone

The expedition got on the move again in mid-July 1805. Now, Lewis and Clark were starting to worry about finding the Shoshone. They needed to trade with them for horses if they were to cross the Rocky Mountains before winter. However, they began to feel better when Sacajawea started to recognize her home territory. On August 12, Lewis, leading a scouting party, reached the tiny stream that is the actual beginning of the Missouri River. One of his men stood with one foot on each side of it. Soon after, the party reached the Continental Divide, the imaginary line running through North America that divides east-flowing from west-flowing rivers. For a moment, Lewis thought he had found the Northwest Passage, but all he saw were more mountains. This ended the last remnants of hope that a Northwest Passage existed as a practical route to the Pacific Ocean.

Near the Lemhi River, a tributary of the Columbia, the expedition finally met up with the Shoshone people. Hostile at first, they were convinced of the explorers' peaceful intent when they saw Sacajawea and her child. Then, most unexpectedly, as Sacajawea sat down with the leaders to translate, she burst into tears. She recognized the chief of the Lemhi Shoshone as her own brother!

There was no way to cross the great falls. They had to build wagons and haul the boats and supplies around the rapids. It took a full month to cover 18 miles (29 kilometers). During this time, Sacajawea became ill with an infection, but was cured by drinking water from a sulfur spring. By the end of July, they reached the site where three streams come together to form the mighty Missouri. Lewis and Clark named them the Jefferson, Madison (after the fourth U.S. president who was then Jefferson's secretary of state), and the Gallatin (after the secretary of the treasury).

After the reunion, the chief sold Lewis and Clark 29 horses and agreed to accompany them partway. With great sadness, Sacajawea left her childhood home behind.

The expedition started again on August 25, 1805, entering what was perhaps the most difficult part of the journey. The trail was steep and crooked and food became so scarce that the group had to eat horse and dog meat. By early September they were able to get some food and more horses from the Flathead people. Then they turned west toward the territory of the Nez Perce (Pierced Nose) people. Trudging through Lolo Pass in the Bitterroot Range, conditions became more desperate. There was snow on all sides and no animals to hunt. Some nights they ate nothing at all. Everyone became weak and ill. Finally, the pathetic-looking group limped into the Nez Perce village where the friendly Indians fed them so well that they got sick again. But all recovered.

The Pacific at last

After building boats, Lewis and Clark floated down the Clearwater River to the Snake, arriving on October 10, 1805. Because they had crossed the Continental Divide, they were no longer in the Louisiana Purchase. This was Oregon country, claimed by both Great Britain and the United States.

On October 16, 1805 the expedition reached the Columbia River. They saw

Shoshone women water their horses.

salmon jumping in the water, but few of the men tried to catch them. Nothing interested them but meat. Along the way they bartered with the native peoples for food. By now, however, the group had very little left to trade. Sometimes Lewis showed off his telescope or one of the men played the violin for dinner.

After passing Mount Hood, the highest point in the Cascade Mountains, Lewis and Clark rowed into the great

A reconstruction of Fort Clatsop was built in 1955.

gorge of the Columbia River. It was the end of October. Suddenly they felt as though they were in a rain forest, with high dense trees lining both sides of the river and the waterfalls filling the air with a fine mist. The Pacific Ocean could not be far away.

At last, three long years since leaving St. Louis, there it was—the Pacific Ocean, which Lewis and Clark first saw on November 7, 1805. Technically, what they saw was a large bay a few miles from the Pacific, which they reached on November 15. After a little time for celebration, work began again. They had to build a winter fort. Now Lewis and Clark did a most unusual thing. They asked for a vote of the group, including Sacajawea, as to the fort's location. It was decided to build the fort on the south shore near present-day Astoria, Oregon.

With help from the Clatsop and Chinook Indians, the expedition passed the winter with a reasonable amount of food and in good health. Lewis worked on his journals, especially detailed descriptions of the various plant and animals species they had seen. Clark worked on his maps, which proved to be surprisingly accurate.

The journey home

The great expedition headed back home on March 13, 1806. They left behind letters for any European traders who might be sailing the coast. The party split up at

Lewis included notes and drawings in his journal.

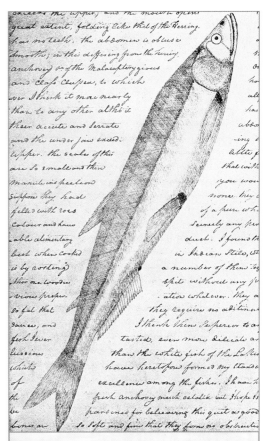

Clark's sketch of a trout is accompanied by notes of his observations.

Bitterroot River in June. Lewis and his group headed north to explore the Marias River. Clark and his group, including Sacajawea, went south to explore the Yellowstone River.

Lewis's exploration was nearly fatal. On August 7 while hunting for food, one of the hunters who was blind in one eye and apparently needed glasses for the other thought Lewis was an elk and shot him in the buttocks. He was disabled and had to lie on his stomach for about a month. Meanwhile, Clark and his group reached the Yellowstone River east of present-day Billings, Montana. There on a gigantic rock outcropping, he carved his name and the date—July 25, 1806. He called it Pompey's Rock for Sacajawea's little boy. Today, it is known as Pompey's Pillar. Sacajawea then led them through Big Hole Pass, a mountain gap near today's Jackson, Wyoming, a shortcut that made the traveling easier.

Lewis and Clark were reunited on the Missouri River and reached the Mandan village in mid-August. They persuaded one of the chiefs, Big White, to return to Washington with them to meet the president. But this was goodbye to Sacajawea, her son, and her husband Charbonneau. He was paid for his services, but Sacajawea, who had meant so much to the expedition, was not. Clark did offer to raise Sacajawea's son when the boy was old enough to leave her.

The exploring party returned to St. Louis on September 23, 1806, to be welcomed by a crowd of 5,000 people.

They stood cheering along the banks. Most people—and for that matter the president of the United States—had given them up for dead. This is the last entry by Clark in the expedition journal: "a fine morning we commenced wrighting & c." From St. Louis, Lewis and Clark went on to Washington, D.C., to report directly to President Jefferson.

When the cheering died

Although they remained close friends, Lewis and Clark went their separate ways after the great expedition. Both men were awarded large land grants in the West. Lewis resigned his army commission and was made governor of the Louisiana Territory in 1808. But as good as he was as an explorer, he was poor as an administrator. He never did adjust to the politician's life. Often moody, he now had times of depression as well.

Lewis never married. In 1809, he was in trouble for poorly prepared financial reports, so he headed to Washington, D.C., to clear his name. He stopped for the night in a boardinghouse in Tennessee and the next morning was found dead of two gunshot wounds. The verdict was suicide, but many experts later questioned whether such a marksman as Lewis would have had to shoot himself twice. Some think one of America's great heroes might have been murdered for his money. Whatever the cause of death, it was a great loss to the young nation. He was only 35 years old.

William Clark was deeply saddened by the death of his close friend. Unlike Lewis, he went on to a successful career. He was named brigadier general of **militia** and superintendent of Indian affairs for the Louisiana Territory. Through all the years of his tenure, he made constant pleas to the governor for fair treatment of native peoples. When part of the Louisiana Territory became the Missouri Territory in 1813, he was appointed governor and served in that job until the territory became the 24th state in 1821. Clark made his home in St. Louis and married his childhood sweetheart, Julia Hancock. After her death, he married a second time, to Harriet Kennerly. In 1814, Clark led an expedition up the Mississippi to the mouth of the Wisconsin River at Prairie du Chien. He was surveyor general for Illinois, Missouri, and Arkansas in 1824–1825 and in 1828 laid out plans for the town of Paducah, Kentucky. At the age of 69, Clark died at the St. Louis home of his eldest son on September 1, 1838. He was buried with military honors.

In addition to raising his own children, Clark made good on his word and raised Sacajawea's son Pomp, whose European name was Jean-Baptiste. He became a fur trader, eventually moved to California, and became mayor of San Luis Rey. He died in 1866.

Lewis and Clark served their president well. They found what was then the most direct route across the new territory of the West. They were the first American citizens to cross the Continental Divide and see the Rocky Mountains. They did not find the Northwest Passage because it did not exist. They completed detailed journals that contained a wealth of information on plant and animal life, including hundreds never before described by science. Lewis compiled several journals of Native American languages. Clark drew the best map to that date of the continent of North America. Even more, they dispelled fear and ignorance of the vast territory beyond the Mississippi and induced more exploration and settlement all the way to the Pacific coast.

In the 21st century it is difficult to imagine the dangers and difficulties faced by Lewis and Clark and the Corps of Discovery. They were out of contact with the eastern part of the continent for three years. Whatever they needed, they had to carry with them. Whatever accident or illness occurred, they had to fix it themselves. They were more alone than a person today can probably imagine. Yet they succeeded. Because of their bravery, survival, and success, we honor "Lewis and Clark, the explorers" as true American heroes.

This portrait depicts William Clark later in his life.

Chapter Six
Zebulon Pike
Where Does the River Begin? (1805–1806)

At first glance, Zebulon Montgomery Pike (1779–1813) does not seem to be much of an explorer. He is actually most famous for what he did not do. He was sent to find the beginnings of the Mississippi River. He incorrectly named Leech Lake as the **source.** He is famous for the Colorado mountain that is named for him—Pikes Peak. But he tried and could not climb it. And after exploring the West, he said that the Great Plains would never be suitable for settlement. Even so, Pike did influence thinking about settlement in the American West for many years after his death.

The army life

Zebulon Pike was born near Trenton, New Jersey, on January 5, 1779. His father had been a major in the American army and continued his career as a regular officer in the new United States Army after the Revolution. Pike also joined the army. At a young age, he was a cadet in his father's company and in 1799, at the age of 20, he was commissioned a lieutenant.

For the next six years, he served at various posts on the frontier. Then, in 1805, General James Wilkinson chose Pike to lead an expedition to find the true source of the Mississippi River. In addition, he was to tell Native Americans in the area that they were now under the control of the

A portrait of Zebulon Pike (1779–1813)

U.S. government. He was also to warn any British fur traders that they were trapping in U.S. territory.

Wilkinson is a controversial figure in American history. He served in the American Revolution, but in 1787 took an oath of allegiance to Spain and became in effect a paid secret agent. However, in 1791 he was granted a commission in the U.S. Army and was named governor of a northern portion of the Louisiana Purchase.

Search for the source

Along with 20 men and supplies for four months, Pike set out in a **keelboat**

from St. Louis on August 9, 1805. Winter threatened to close in when he neared the Falls of St. Anthony (now Minneapolis) in Minnesota. But he decided to chance the weather, and in December, he left some of his men behind in a hastily built stockade. Hauling supplies on a **sledge,** he and the rest of the party tried to find the source of the Mississippi. When they reached Leech Lake in northern Minnesota, Pike decided he had done it.

Pike was mistaken. The true source is now agreed to be Lake Itasca in Minnesota, only about 30 miles (145 kilometers) from Leech Lake. But Pike was satisfied that he had completed his mission. He returned to St. Louis on April 30, 1806.

The strange mission

Within a few months of his return, Pike got orders from Wilkinson for a second expedition. But historians find this mission a somewhat strange one. Pike was to find the headwaters of the Arkansas and Red Rivers. He was also supposed to find out what he could about any Spanish settlements in New Mexico. In other words, Pike was supposed to be a sort of spy while wandering around the area and perhaps getting lost in Spanish territory. What Wilkinson hoped to gain from this is not clear. Even stranger, there is reason to believe that Wilkinson secretly let the Spanish know of Pike's expedition.

Pike was well aware that relations between Spain and the young United States had never been particularly good. But he was too obedient an officer to ask too many questions of his superior. So, on July 15, 1806, he set out from St. Louis with 23 men, including Wilkinson's own son and Dr. John Robinson, who worked for Wilkinson. First, they traveled to Osage villages on what is now the western border of

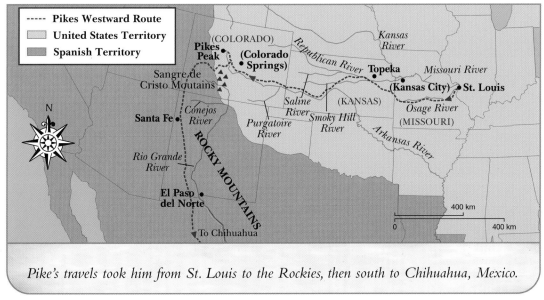

Pike's travels took him from St. Louis to the Rockies, then south to Chihuahua, Mexico.

Missouri. They brought home some captive members of the Osage people. Next, they **trekked** north to Nebraska into the land of the Pawnee. But this time they were met with a hostile reception. Pike did not know it, but probably acting on a message from Wilkinson, Don Facundo Melgares had earlier led a Spanish force of about 600 men into Pawnee territory. Melgares warned the Pawnee not to deal with the Americans.

Pike left the Pawnee and in late September turned south toward the Arkansas River. He was following the obvious trail that Melgares and his men had left. Reaching the river, Pike sent Wilkinson's son and six men back to St. Louis to report on the mission thus far. With the rest of his party, he turned west toward the Rockies, which they sighted on November 15. One tall mountain caught their attention and since it seemed to be close, they headed toward it. But it was November 23 before they even got close.

Pike judged that it would take only one more day to reach the base. With three other men, he set out to climb what he called Great Mountain.

But Pike had misjudged much about the great mountain—how far away it was, how rugged the surrounding terri-

Pike nears the Rockies on his second expedition in 1806.

Pike himself never reached the summit of Pikes Peak.

tory was, and its height. That was especially unfortunate because the expedition party was wearing summer uniforms and had brought no others. For three and a half days and once during a raging snowstorm, Pike and his men tried to climb the mountain. Finally, he gave up. They were, however, able to climb the smaller Cheyenne Peak, about 15 miles (24 kilometers) in the distance. The mountain he could not climb was later named Pikes Peak.

In the month of December, Pike explored Colorado as far north as the **source** of the South Platte River and as far south as the Sangre de Cristo Mountains. In January, near the Royal **Gorge** of the Arkansas River, he built a small fort where he could leave his men who were ill. He left the fort with thirteen men on January 14, 1807.

In the cold of midwinter, Pike and the small group made a difficult crossing of the Sangre de Cristo Mountains in southern Colorado. The weather was so frigid that some of the group suffered frostbite, two so badly that their feet had to be amputated. The men had to be left behind, but Pike promised that they would be rescued. According to reports, he made good on that promise.

The rest of the party traveled to Rio Conejos, a tributary of the Rio Grande, where they built a small fort out of

Zebulon Pike was killed during the Battle of York in 1813.

cottonwood logs. They were now in Spanish-held New Mexico. In early February, Dr. Robinson left the group for Santa Fe, where he said he had to collect a fur-trading debt. Instead, he reached Santa Fe and told the Spanish where Pike was camped. On February 26, 1807 the Spanish calvary arrived at the fort to arrest Pike for being in their territory. Supposedly, Pike said to them, "Is this not the Red River?"—meaning that he thought he was in U.S. territory. However, most now believe Pike that knew exactly where he was and was simply carrying out his orders of spying on the Spanish.

Many think that Zebulon Pike had every intention of being captured by the Spanish. Perhaps so, because during the year he spent as their prisoner, he was able to observe the number and types of troops that Spain had in its territory.

Pike and his men were taken as prisoners to Santa Fe, where Melgares took over and escorted the group to Chihuahua in Mexico. They were exceptionally well treated. Pike did manage to hide some of his notes in his gun barrel and he memorized as much as he could of Spanish holdings. After about a year, Pike was escorted back over the border and released at Natchitoches, Louisiana.

Into the history books

Pike was in some trouble when he returned to the United States because his name was now tied to Wilkinson's. But he was absolved of any blame in whatever Wilkinson had been trying to do.

In 1808, Pike was promoted to major and then to colonel in 1812, when war broke out between the United States and Great Britain. Made a brigadier general in 1813, he led the attack on York (present-day Toronto), Canada. With heavy rifle fire pouring down on his troops from the heavily defended town, Pike took personal charge of the assault. The British were forced to retreat. But as they did, they exploded their powder magazine. The horrendous blast killed 52 Americans and 40 British soldiers. In addition, 180 U.S. soldiers were wounded, Zebulon Pike among them. His spine was broken.

In great agony, he was moved to the flagship Madison where a captured British flag was placed beneath his head. Pike died on April 27, 1813.

Pike's report of his **trek** to Minnesota, *An Account of Expeditions to the **Sources** of the Mississippi,* and of his march to Santa Fe were published before his death. They were rather poorly put together and were less accurate and far less helpful than the journals of Lewis and Clark. He judged that the American West, especially the Southwest, was basically unfit for settlement. He thought that a Southwest Passage might be the best route to the Pacific Ocean. Such views played a large role in shaping American ideas on expanding into these areas over the next several years.

Today, Pikes Peak in the Rocky Mountains near Pueblo, Colorado, is a favorite tourist attraction. It is one of only two of the state's mountains over 14,000 feet (4,267 meters) high that have roads all the way to the top. Pikes Peak Toll Road was opened in 1916. A train, built in 1891, also runs to the top. The first man to climb the peak was Dr. Edwin James in 1820. The first woman was Julia Archibald Holmes in 1858. Author Katherine Lee Bates thought the view from Pikes Peak was so extraordinary that she was inspired to write "America the Beautiful" in 1893. For those who want to climb the mountain today, Barr Trail is 13 winding miles (21 kilometers) and ascends 7,500 vertical feet (2,286 meters) to the top. Pike would be quite surprised by all this activity. After his failure, he predicted that no one would ever reach the top of his mountain.

Chapter Seven

Manuel Lisa
Across the Wide Missouri (1807)

He was more fur trapper than explorer, but his explorations in the Pacific Northwest helped to open the Missouri River area to white settlers in the early 1800s. Manuel Lisa (1772–1820) was a Spaniard born in New Orleans on September 8, 1772. His father had come to America years earlier from Murcia, Spain, and his mother had been born in St. Augustine, Florida.

The fur trade

As a young man, probably about 1790, Lisa went to St. Louis. Before long, he established himself in the flourishing fur trade. He was so successful that in 1802 Spain awarded him a **patent** granting him a monopoly for trade with the Osage people. The monopoly ended the following year, however, because the United States bought the Louisiana Territory from France, who had bought it from Spain. Lisa lost the monopoly but gained automatic U.S. citizenship as a resident of the new territory.

About the year 1806, Lisa formed an organization with several St. Louis fur traders and made several river expeditions. In 1807, he led 42 men up the Missouri River where they built trading posts and forts.

On November 21, 1807, Lisa built a trading house at the mouth of the Big Horn River in what is now Montana. In the spring he set up a fort nearby and named it Fort Raymond for his son. Lisa had earlier married Mary Charles with whom he had three children, who all died young. The fort was later called Fort Manuel, and it was the first such structure on the upper Missouri River. Lisa returned from the fort in the summer of 1808 to form the Missouri Fur Company along with several traders.

The first expedition for the Missouri Fur Company began in June 1809 when about 350 men, Americans and French Canadians, left St. Louis with Lisa as one of the leaders. They built Fort Lisa about 12 miles beyond the mouth of the Big Knife River in present-day North Dakota. Lisa sent a small group to explore the Three Forks area of the Missouri before he returned to St. Louis that October.

When no word was heard from the group by spring of 1811, Lisa set out to look for them with 25 men in what was to be a legendary "race." The river barge carrying Lisa's search party overtook the flotilla of another trader, John Jacob Astor, at the Niobrara River, which flows into the Missouri in northeastern Nebraska. Although Hunt had about a three week's start, Lisa's barge overtook him on June 2 just beyond the mouth of the Niobrara. It turned out to be a friendly race, and both expeditions went on their way.

Map

Three Forks
Gallatin River
Jefferson River
Madison River
Yellowstone Lake
(MONTANA)
Missouri River
Yellowstone River
Bighorn River
BIGHORN MOUNTAINS
Powder River
Fort Raymond
Tongue River
Knife River
(Bismarck)
(NORTH DAKOTA)
Grand River
(SOUTH DAKOTA)
(Pierre)
White River
Niobrara River
(WYOMING)
(NEBRASKA)
Missouri River
St. Louis
N

Legend:
- Lisa's Route
- United States Territory
- Oregon Country

200 km
0   200 Miles

Lisa explored the Missouri River from St. Louis to Montana.

Agent for Native American affairs

Lisa was later named governor of the Missouri Territory and was subagent for native peoples on the Missouri above the mouth of the Kansas River. Until his death in 1820, Lisa made at least a dozen trips on the Missouri, traveling at least 26,000 miles (41,843 kilometers).

Lisa married twice more, having two more children. On his last expedition he stayed at another Fort Lisa, built in 1812 near present-day Omaha, Nebraska. This Fort Lisa became the most important trading post on the Missouri River between 1813 and 1822.

Manuel Lisa died in St. Louis on August 12, 1820. Without much fanfare, he had opened the Missouri River area to white traders and settlers during the early 1800s.

Chapter Eight

Peter Skene Ogden:
Tough Man in the Northwest (1824–1830)

Explorer and trader Peter Skene Ogden (1794–1854) owns two well-deserved reputations. As an explorer, he was a major figure in the opening of the American West, especially the Snake River country. That included parts of present-day Washington, Oregon, California, Nevada, Utah, Idaho, and Montana. He was apparently the first white man to see the Humboldt River in present-day Nevada. As a fur trader, he was said to be the most ruthless of any in a notoriously ruthless business, a man who would stop at nothing, including murder, to reach his goals. In fact, he was once indicted for killing a man who traded with one of his competitors.

The trade business

Peter Ogden was born in 1794 in Quebec City, Canada. When he was four years old, the family moved to Montreal where his father had been appointed a judge. Ogden's parents hoped he would become a lawyer, as had his father, grandfather, and eventually his brothers. But Ogden had other ideas. Law seemed too tame a career. At the time Montreal was the center of the North American fur-trading business. This adventurous, dangerous existence appealed to young Ogden. When he was seventeen he joined the North West

A portrait of Peter Skene Ogden (1794–1854)

Company. Rivalry was sharp and bitter between Montreal-based North West and the Hudson's Bay Company, controlled from London. Until 1821 when the two companies **merged,** Ogden was in the center of this murderous rivalry.

Earning a reputation

Stationed at Ile-à-la-Crosse in what is now Saskatchewan, Ogden made rapid advancement at North West, being given a partnership after nine years. Not only did he prove his ability as a leader, but he quickly earned a reputation as one of the most violent and ruthless of all traders. In fact, through this period he was accused of several crimes. In March 1818, he was actually indicted for murder. It was said he had killed a Native American who had traded with the Hudson's Bay Company instead of North West. To escape jail time or worse, North West sent Ogden to a remote outpost in the Pacific Northwest.

Finally, North West and Hudson's Bay decided it would be a smarter financial move to merge and bankrupt the rest of the **competition.** They joined forces in 1821 under the Hudson's Bay name, but that was not a good move for Ogden. His reputation was so notorious that none of the directors wanted to employ him any longer. Ogden went back to Montreal and then to London to try to persuade Hudson's Bay to rehire him. No one would.

Then in a stroke of luck, Ogden's bad image actually worked in his favor. Hudson's Bay sent George Simpson to what is now British Columbia, Washington, Oregon, and Idaho to do some-

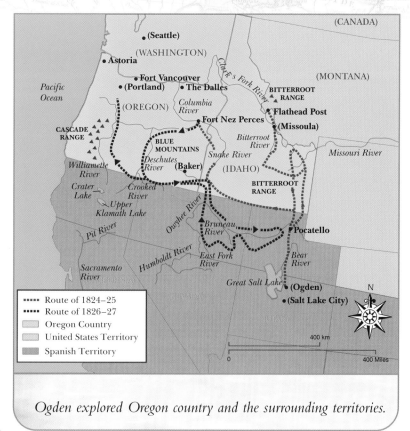

Ogden explored Oregon country and the surrounding territories.

thing about the poor performance of the company's posts in that region. The job had added hazards beyond fur trading. This territory was being disputed by the United States and Great Britain; it was not settled until 1846. Just to the south was Spanish-held land. There was danger to fur traders everywhere. In fact, so far the experience of trapping in the Snake River region had been extremely expensive and dangerous. No one wanted the job of leading the expeditions. Then Simpson had an idea. He would bring in the most ruthless, no-nonsense man for the job. Peter Ogden, at age 30, qualified. He is said to have accepted the post with "the utmost readiness." In that manner in 1823 Ogden was back on the payroll, posted to Spokane House in eastern Washington.

In the spring of 1824, Ogden received instructions to go on a fur-trapping expedition in the area around the Snake River in present-day Idaho. He was instructed to get every beaver **pelt** he could trap. If that meant ridding the regions of all the beavers, that was all right with Hudson's Bay. The company figured that sooner or later the United States was going to try to take over the disputed Oregon Territory. If so, it was in the interest of Hudson's Bay—a British firm—to take every pelt it could while it had the chance.

Ogden left Flathead House at Flathead Lake in northern Montana on December 20, 1824. This was no small scouting party expedition. With him went 58 men, 61 guns, 268 horses, and 352 traps. In addition, there were 30 women and 35 children, 10 slaves, and 53 freemen. The women's main job was to skin and prepare the pelts. Besides the beaver, the men had to hunt elk, deer, and buffalo, because they had to find food to eat. Hudson's Bay believed that these expeditions should "live off the land."

It was during this expedition that one of Ogden's men caught sight of the Great Salt Lake while scaling a peak. He was probably the second Westerner to have seen it. Ogden also reached the river in Utah that now bears his name.

In 1825–1826, Ogden explored south through eastern Oregon to Malheur Lake and Klamath Lake in northern California. Before he returned north, he named Mount Shasta, which is the tallest peak in the southern Cascade Range.

The last expedition

Peter Ogden's most important expeditions were also his last, during 1828–1829. He traveled south into Nevada where he found a river he named "Unknown." Famed American explorer John Charles Fremont later named the river after German explorer Alexander von Humboldt, who had never seen it. Oddly enough, the Humboldt River, which should have been named for Ogden, became an important marker that led American settlers to California. Ogden traveled the Humboldt to its **source** in the Humboldt Sinks, a series of marshy lakes east of present-day Reno. At the Sinks, he had a serious clash with Native American tribes.

From the Sinks, Ogden and party turned south until they reached the Colorado River. Somewhere near present-day Needles, California, they had a skirmish with the Mojave people but fought them off with guns and spears. Then Ogden followed the Colorado all the way to the Gulf of California, thus becoming the first non-Native American to cross the American West from north to south.

Unfortunately, there are no journals from this wide-ranging expedition. On the return trip north, Ogden crossed the mountains at Cajon Pass near San Bernardino, California. This led him into the San Joaquin Valley. Back on the Columbia River near The Dalles, Oregon, nine men were drowned when a boat, also carrying Ogden's journals, capsized and was lost.

Although none of his journeys was as important as his last, Ogden spent the next 24 years in the fur trade. First he was superintendent of trade in the British Columbia area, then chief agent in 1835, and finally a principal officer in the Hudson Bay Company in 1845. Although his competitors and even those who worked with him called him "one of the most unprincipled men" in the region, he polished his unsavory reputation somewhat in 1847. He rescued survivors of the Whitman Massacre in 1847 when missionary Marcus Whitman, his wife, and other party members were killed by Cayuse natives near Walla Walla, Washington.

Ogden always remained a British subject and spoke French as fluently as English. He was twice married to Native American women and knew a number of native languages. His numerous expeditions expanded what was known of the American West. Even so, there is no denying that Peter Skene Ogden was a tough man in a tough trade.

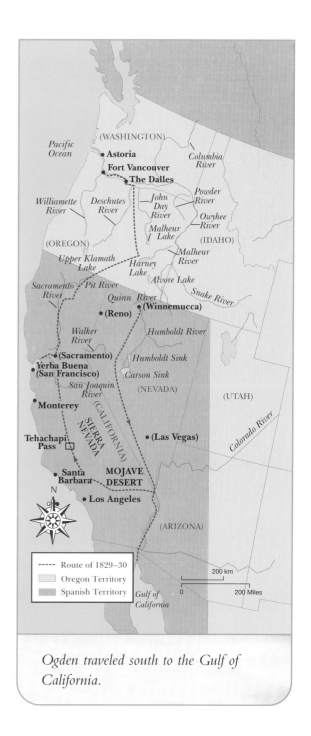

Ogden traveled south to the Gulf of California.

Epilogue:

What Did They Find?

In the 1600s, explorers of the Pacific Northwest were trying to find out just where it was and what it was. Was it hooked onto the continent of Asia? Was there a great waterway to the Pacific? When these questions were answered with no and no, those who explored the Northwest in the 1700s and 1800s began to look at what was inside the territory they knew existed.

These explorers were a mixture of the old and new. Men such as Bering and Vancouver were adventurers in the old seafaring spirit of Columbus and Magellan. They boldly sailed their ships into the unknown, charting new territory, erasing old fears. Men such as Lewis and Clark and Mackenzie were adventurers, too, no less bold or daring because their ships were canoes and **keelboats** and their "ocean voyage" was through the muddy waters of the Missouri or down a northern river into the Arctic Ocean. But like Vancouver, the main objective of Lewis and Clark was to bring back detailed, scientific records of their journeys.

This was also the time for a different kind of explorer—the businessman, so to speak. These were men such as Lisa and Ogden. They were fur trappers first and explorers second. In seeking fur **pelts** and profits for themselves and their companies, they explored new territory and opened the vast western lands to settlers. The fact that profit, not exploration, was their motive does not make them less effective or important. It took many kinds of people, but adventurers and explorers all, to open up the then unknown and still spectacular territory that is the North American Northwest.

Important Events in the Exploration of the Pacific Northwest

1725	Vitus Bering leaves St. Petersburg, Russia, to explore Russian coast and Alaska, February 5
1730	Bering returns to St. Petersburg after sailing through Bering **Strait** to Arctic Ocean, March
1733	Bering leads Great Northern Expedition to map coasts of Siberia and Alaska; explores Gulf of Alaska, sights Mt. St. Elias
1741	Bering dies of **scurvy** on island named for him, December 8; he is reburied on the island in 1992
1789	Alexander Mackenzie explores river named for him to Arctic Ocean while searching for the Northwest Passage, June–September
1790	Gray is first U.S. citizen to sail around the world
1772–75	George Vancouver sails to South Pacific on second voyage of Captain James Cook
1776–79	Vancouver accompanies Cook on third and last voyage to the Pacific
1791	Robert Gray sails from London to explore the Pacific Northwest, September
1791–94	Vancouver maps more than 1,700 miles of Pacific coastline from San Francisco to British Columbia; misses mouth of Columbia River
1792	Gray becomes first American to explore the Columbia River, in May
1792–93	Mackenzie reaches Pacific coast on second expedition; becomes first U.S. citizen to cross North American continent overland north of Mexico
1803	France sells Louisiana Territory to the United States, in April; Thomas Jefferson makes plans for exploration of the vast region; great overland expedition by Meriwether Lewis and William Clark to the Pacific Ocean is authorized, July 2
1804	Lewis and Clark expedition begins, May 14; first and only fatality occurs, August 20; Sacajawea joins expedition at Fort Mandan
1805	Lewis and Clark reach great falls of the Missouri River, July; Zebulon Pike leads unsuccessful attempt to find **source** of Mississippi River, August 9; Lewis and Clark reach Continental Divide, August 12; Columbia River, October 16; and Pacific Ocean, November 7
1806	Lewis and Clark return to St. Louis, September 23; Pike makes unsuccessful attempt to climb mountain later named for him, November 23
1807	Manuel Lisa explores Missouri River region
1824	Peter Ogden leads expedition to Snake River region
1825–26	Ogden explores Oregon and northern California, names Mount Shasta
1828–29	Ogden explores Nevada, follows Colorado River to Gulf of California

Glossary

bonanza exceptionally large ore discovery, or in general, an extremely large amount of something that is discovered unexpectedly

campaign series of operations to bring about a desired result, such as a military campaign

channel bed for a natural stream of water; deeper part of a river; narrow sea between two land masses

competition contest between rivals

cove small, sheltered inlet

gorge narrow, steep-walled passage, usually of a river, through land

inlet recess in the shore of a sea, lake, or river

keelboat shallow riverboat used for hauling supplies

merge any method of combining two or more organizations

militia part of organized armed forces to be called only in emergency

patent official document conferring a right or privilege

pelt skin with its wool or hair

sandbar ridge of sand built by currents, especially in a river of coastal waters

scurvy disease caused by lack of ascorbic acid (vitamin C), marked by spongy gums, loosening teeth, and bleeding into the skin

sledge vehicles used for transporting heavy loads over snow

sloop small boat with one mast

sound long, broad inlet of the ocean usually parallel to the coast

source beginning of a river

strait narrow passageway connecting two bodies of water

survey to determine data about a tract of land by scientific measurements

trek journey usually involving difficulty or danger

Further Reading

Baker, Daniel. *Explorers and Discoverers of the World*. Detroit: Gale, 1993.

Dietrich, William. *Northwest Passage: The Great Columbia River*. New York: Simon & Schuster, 1995.

Gale Research Group. *Encyclopedia of World Biography*. Detroit: Gale, 2001.

Molzahn, Arlene Bourgeois. *Lewis and Clark: American Explorers*. Berkeley Heights, N.J.: Enslow, 2003.

Witteman, Barbara. *Zebulon Pike: Soldier and Explorer*. Minnetonka, Minn.: Capstone Press, 2002.

Xydes, Georgia. *Alexander Mackenzie and the Explorers of Canada*. Broomall, Pa.: Chelsea House, 1992.

Index